Mommy, Will You Rub My Feet?

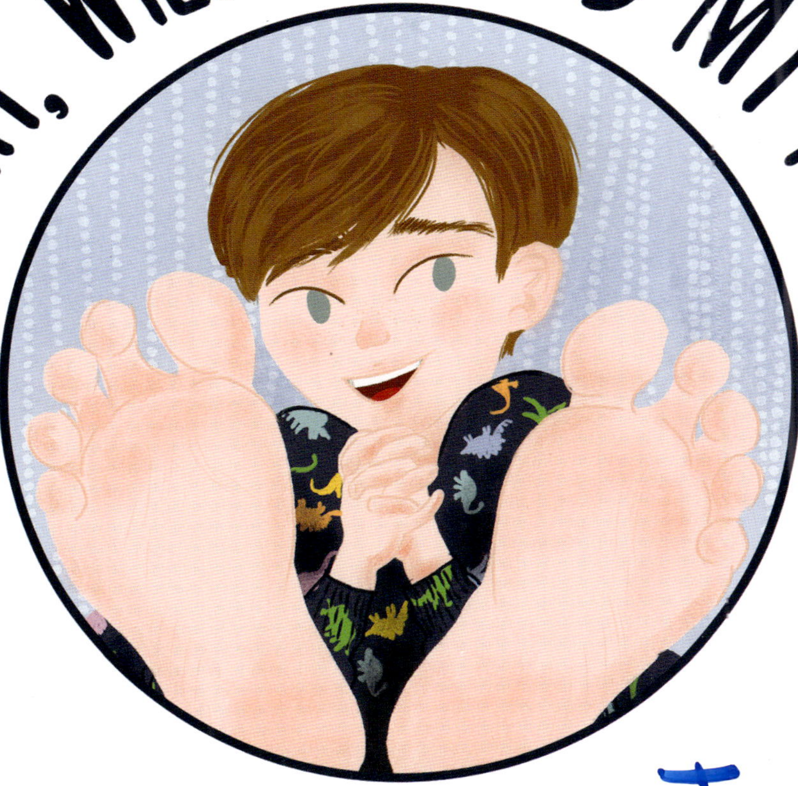

Jessica Jones

Illustrated by Susana Ramírez Solís

© 2024, Jessica Jones

All rights reserved. No part of this book may be used or reproduced in any manner without written permission except in the case of brief quotations embodied in critical articles or reviews.

This is a work of fiction. Any similarity to real persons, living or dead, is coincidental and not intended by the author.

Mommy, Will You Rub My Feet?

Brown Books Kids
Dallas / New York
www.BrownBooksKids.com
(972) 381-0009

A New Era in Publishing®

Publisher's Cataloging-In-Publication Data

Names: Jones, Jessica, 1982- author. | Ramírez Solís, Susana, illustrator.
Title: Mommy, will you rub my feet? / Jessica Jones ; illustrated by Susana Ramírez Solís.
Description: Dallas ; New York : Brown Books Kids, [2024] | Interest age level: 004-008. | Summary: Even after completing his usual getting-ready-for-bed routine, Taj can't fall asleep. He tosses and turns and watches his clock, but nothing works. He goes to Mommy to figure out what's wrong, because the aches and pains he feels aren't like the usual scrapes and bruises from playing outside. In Mommy, Will You Rub My Feet?, debut author Jessica Jones helps parents and children learn to identify growing pains.--Publisher.
Identifiers: ISBN 9781612546629 (hardcover) | LCCN 2024930070
Subjects: LCSH: Mother and child--Juvenile fiction. | Bedtime--Juvenile fiction. | Pain in children--Juvenile fiction. | Foot--Massage--Juvenile fiction. | Emotions--Juvenile fiction. | Sleep--Juvenile fiction. | CYAC: Mother and child--Fiction. | Bedtime--Fiction. | Pain--Fiction. | Foot--Fiction. | Emotions--Fiction. | Sleep--Fiction. | BISAC: JUVENILE FICTION / Social Themes / New Experience. | JUVENILE FICTION / Social Themes / Emotions & Feelings.
Classification: LCC: PZ7.1.J697 Mo 2024 | DDC: [E]--dc23

This book has been officially leveled by using the F&P Text Level Gradient™ Leveling System.

ISBN 978-1-61254-662-9
LCCN 2024930070

Printed in China
10 9 8 7 6 5 4 3 2 1

For more information or to contact the author, please go to
www.JessicaJonesBooks.com

DEDICATION

To Bo, my soulmate. You believed in my vision when no one else did.
And to Taj and Ruby. This is for you.
I love you.

ACKNOWLEDGMENTS

First and foremost, I would not be the woman I am today if it wasn't for my mother. Thank you, Marm, for all the support and love you've provided. You're my best friend, and I recognize and appreciate all the sacrifices you made for me.

I would also like to thank Milli Brown, Brittany Griffiths, Deb Greenberg, and the entire Brown Books Publishing Group team for helping me develop this book.

Every night, after a fun-filled day of adventures,
Taj starts his getting-ready-for-bed routine.

First, he hops into a warm bubble bath …

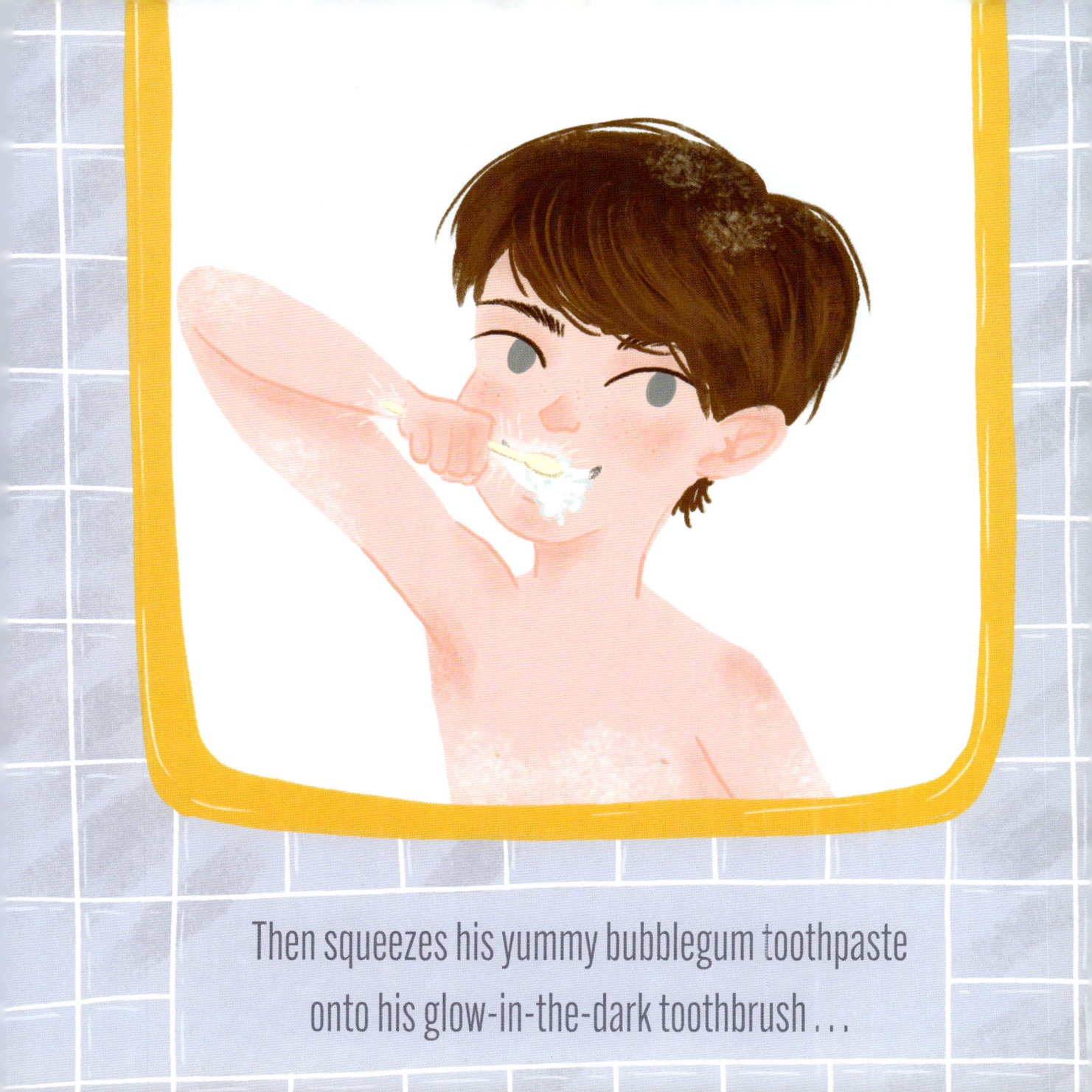

Then squeezes his yummy bubblegum toothpaste onto his glow-in-the-dark toothbrush ...

Next, he yanks on his cozy dinosaur pj's . . .

Finally, he climbs onto a soft and snug gray rocking chair for his favorite part of the day: reading bedtime stories with his mommy.

"Can we read the book about the tree and the boy? And the one about the fish who has a pout?" Taj asks, hugging two of his favorite books.

"Of course," his mommy replies.

As they begin to read the book about the tree and the boy, she stops suddenly. "Woah!" she says as she touches her belly.

"What's the matter, Mommy?" Taj asks.

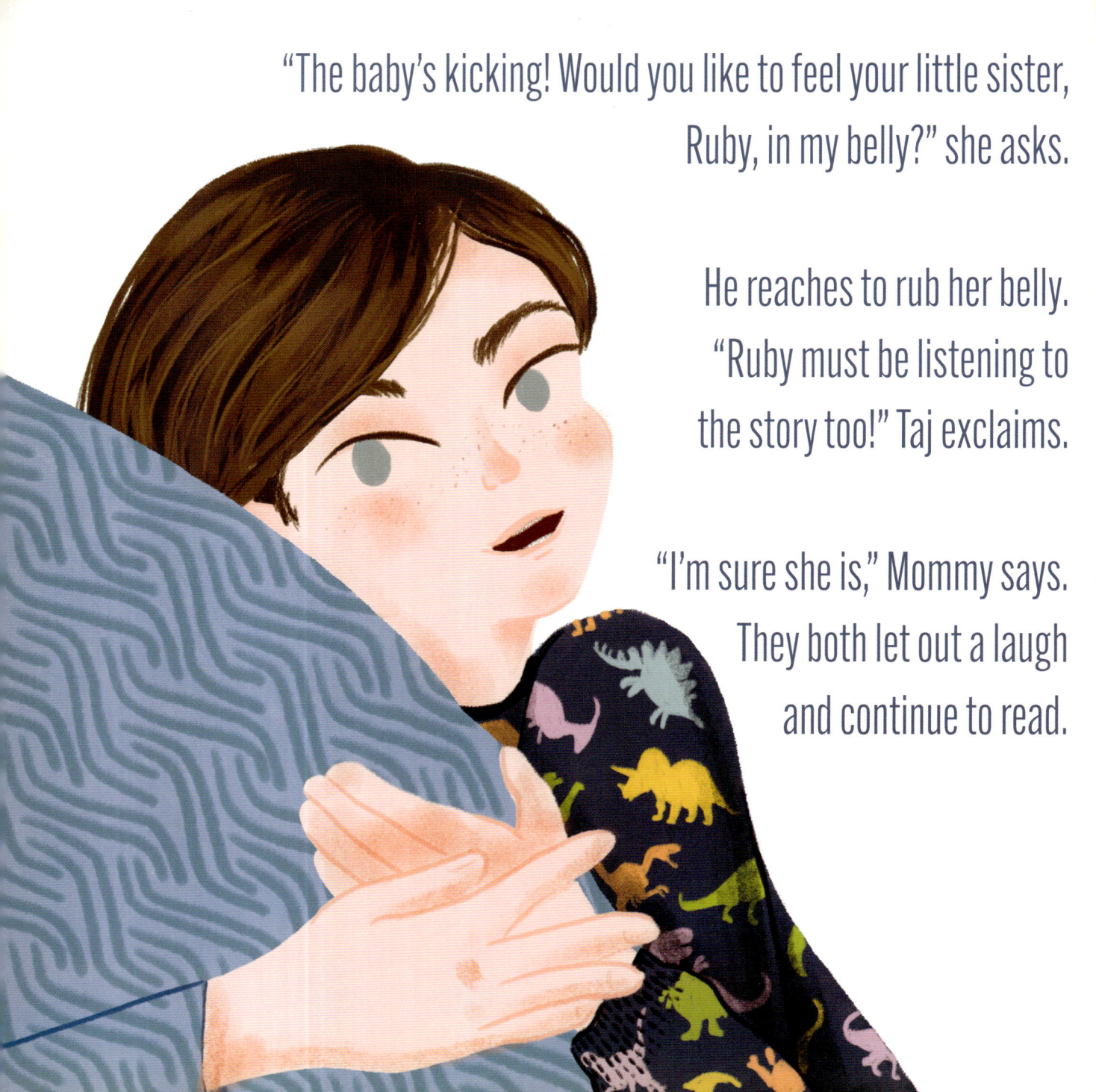

"The baby's kicking! Would you like to feel your little sister, Ruby, in my belly?" she asks.

He reaches to rub her belly. "Ruby must be listening to the story too!" Taj exclaims.

"I'm sure she is," Mommy says. They both let out a laugh and continue to read.

When they finish the two books, Taj climbs onto his Mommy's back, and she piggybacks him to his bedroom. He jumps into his bed, and she pulls his superhero bedsheet over his legs, tummy, and shoulders, making sure he is tucked in tight. Then she leans over and kisses his forehead. While quietly leaving his room, she whispers, "Don't let the bed bugs bite."

As Taj closes his eyes, his feet and legs start to throb. He tries to relax, but the pain doesn't go away. After tossing and turning, he opens his eyes and stares at his shark-shaped ticktock clock hanging on the wall. He waits. And waits. And waits to fall asleep until finally he slowly climbs out of bed, tiptoes down the hall, and heads into Mommy's bedroom.

"Mommy, I'm not feeling well," Taj says softly.

She gently rubs his back and says, "Come on back up and sit next to me." While rocking him back and forth on the soft and snug gray rocking chair, she looks and feels for anything out of place.

"You don't have a fever, your nose isn't running, your throat isn't swollen, and you're not coughing.

"What are you feeling?" she asks.

"Well, it starts at my feet. They kind of... hurt a little," Taj attempts to explain. "And my legs are sore too," he continues. "I didn't fall today, so I don't know why they hurt."

"Hmm, that is odd," she says. "I'm sure we can figure this out together."

"Okay, Mommy. But it feels like the soreness is on the inside."

Without skipping a beat, she knows what he is feeling. Her eyes grow wide as she looks at her son.

"Ohhh, you mean you're having growing pains."

"What are growing pains?"
Taj asks with a puzzled look.

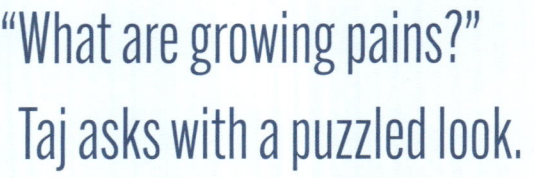

"Growing pains are normal, and many children your age experience them. When you jump, climb, and run around all day, your muscles and joints get tired."

"Oh, so I didn't do anything wrong?"

"No, not at all. Your body is telling you that you're exhausted and need some rest!" she exclaims.

"I had growing pains at your age and understand what you're going through," Mommy says. "I know just the right remedies to soothe them."

But as she goes to get a warm towel and heating pad, Taj looks at her and says…

She turns, looks at him, and smiles. Without saying a word, she sits back down and begins to rub his feet, his legs, then back down to his toes. Taj giggles as she starts "This Little Piggy." Within minutes, he is relaxed, comfortable, and fast asleep.

As she lays him back down in his bed, she reflects on the many times he's come to her for guidance, and she realizes their special bond.

"I'll always be here for you," she whispers.

A couple years later...